EVERYTHING IS STREAMING

MUSIC, MOVIES, AND MORE

EMMETT MARTIN

Please visit our website, www.garethstevens.com.
For a free color catalog of all our high-quality books,
call toll free 1-800-542-2595 or fax 1-877-542-2596.

Portions of this work were originally authored by Peg Robinson and published as *How Streaming Works* (Everyday STEM). All new material in this edition authored by Emmett Martin.

Library of Congress Cataloging-in-Publication Data
Names: Martin, Emmett, author.
Title: Everything is streaming : music, movies, and more / Emmett Martin.
Description: New York : Gareth Stevens Publishing, [2023] | Series: STEM is
    everywhere! | Includes bibliographical references and index.
Identifiers: LCCN 2022021739 (print) | LCCN 2022021740 (ebook) | ISBN
    9781538283493 (library binding) | ISBN 9781538283479 (paperback) | ISBN
    9781538283509 (ebook)
Subjects: LCSH: Streaming technology (Telecommunications)–Juvenile
    literature.
Classification: LCC TK5105.386 .M376 2023 (print) | LCC TK5105.386
    (ebook) | DDC 006.7/876–dc23/eng/20220707
LC record available at https://lccn.loc.gov/2022021739
LC ebook record available at https://lccn.loc.gov/2022021740

Published in 2023 by
Gareth Stevens Publishing
2544 Clinton Street
Buffalo, NY 14224

Copyright © 2023 Gareth Stevens Publishing

Designer: Tanya Dellaccio
Editor: Therese Shea

Photo credits: Series Art Supphachai Salaeman/Shutterstock.com; cover Said Marroun/Shutterstock.com; p. 4 Piotr Piatrouski/Shutterstock. com; p. 5 Sevastsyanau Uladzimir/Shutterstock.com; p. 7 (top) naluwan/Shutterstock.com; p. 7 (bottom) Monkey Business Images/ Shutterstock.com; p. 8 NicoElNino/Shutterstock.com; p. 9 selinofoto/Shutterstock.com; p. 11 Chunumunu/iStock.com; p. 13 Travelpixs/ Shutterstock.com; p. 14 DenPhotos/Shutterstock.com; p. 15 Vink Fan/Shutterstock.com; p. 17 sirtravelalot/Shutterstock.com; p. 19 Rido/ Shutterstock.com; p. 21 (top) Proxima Studio/Shutterstock.com; p. 21 (bottom) pixinoo/Shutterstock.com; p. 22 Justlight/Shutterstock.co; p. 23 Cassiano Correia/Shutterstock.com; p. 25 (top) Indypenden/Shutterstock.com; p 25 (bottom) mohammed.yousuf/Shutterstock.com; p. 27 art.em.po/Shutterstock.com.

Printed in the United States of America

CPSIA compliance information: Batch #CWGS23: For further information contact Gareth Stevems Publishing at 1-800-398-2504.

Find us on

CONTENTS

Words in the glossary appear in **bold** type
the first time they are used in the text.

THE STREAMING LIFE

When was the last time you streamed a video or music? It probably wasn't too long ago! These days, streaming **media** like TV shows, movies, **podcasts**, and videos is something we don't even think about. We stream through our smartphones, computers, TVs, and tablets. We do it to entertain ourselves, to stay in touch with family and friends, and to get up-to-date news.

EARLY DAYS OF ONLINE MUSIC

DO YOU EVER WATCH YOUR FAVORITE BANDS PERFORM ONLINE? ON JUNE 24, 1993, THE BAND SEVERE TIRE DAMAGE WAS THE FIRST TO PERFORM LIVE ON THE INTERNET. THE BAND, WHICH INCLUDED COMPUTER SCIENTISTS AND ENGINEERS, WAS THE OPENING ACT FOR THE ROLLING STONES WHEN THEY PERFORMED LIVE ONLINE THE FOLLOWING YEAR.

TWITCH IS A SERVICE THAT HELPS GAMERS LIVESTREAM THEIR VIDEOS. LIVESTREAM MEANS SENDING OR RECEIVING VIDEO AND AUDIO OVER THE INTERNET AS AN EVENT IS HAPPENING.

Streaming is so much a part of daily life that we might only think about the **technology** that makes it happen when it doesn't work. In this book, you'll learn what's actually happening when we stream something—

WHAT *IS* STREAMING?

Streaming is a way of sending data so that the computer can begin processing it before the whole file is sent. When you download a file, you move it from somewhere else to your computer. Ordinary downloads are kept in **permanent** memory, or storage on the computer. Large files can take up a lot of memory.

When you stream a file, you use it right away, even while it's downloading. Then, the computer "forgets it" instead of storing it. This allows people to watch movies, listen to music, or play games. Your computer doesn't hold entire movies, songs, or games if it streams them.

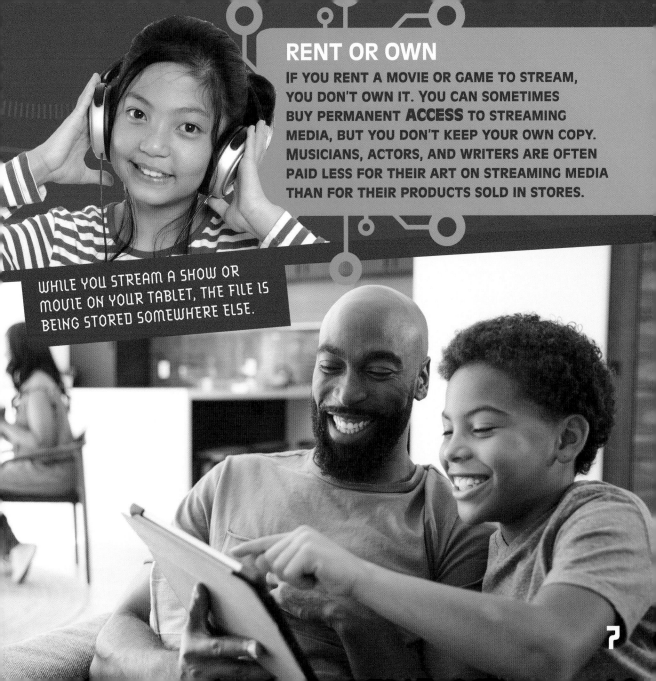

RENT OR OWN

IF YOU RENT A MOVIE OR GAME TO STREAM, YOU DON'T OWN IT. YOU CAN SOMETIMES BUY PERMANENT **ACCESS** TO STREAMING MEDIA, BUT YOU DON'T KEEP YOUR OWN COPY. MUSICIANS, ACTORS, AND WRITERS ARE OFTEN PAID LESS FOR THEIR ART ON STREAMING MEDIA THAN FOR THEIR PRODUCTS SOLD IN STORES.

WHILE YOU STREAM A SHOW OR MOVIE ON YOUR TABLET, THE FILE IS BEING STORED SOMEWHERE ELSE.

BITS AND PIECES

At first, data files like movies and TV shows were treated as whole chunks of information, or data. It took a lot of computer space to make room for these files. And you couldn't watch them until the whole file was downloaded. This could take some time, depending on the size of the file and the speed of the internet.

DATA DECISIONS

YOU MAY ALREADY THINK THAT STREAMING IS BETTER THAN DOWNLOADING. HOWEVER, IF YOU HAVE A LIMITED DATA PLAN FOR YOUR SMARTPHONE, STREAMING A MOVIE CAN QUICKLY USE UP YOUR DATA IF YOU'RE NOT CONNECTED TO Wi-Fi. WATCHING A MOVIE ALREADY DOWNLOADED ON YOUR PHONE WON'T USE UP ANY OF YOUR DATA.

Then, someone got a clever idea. Instead of sending a whole movie file, for example, the file was chopped up into much smaller bits of data. You could begin to watch the movie as soon as your computer processed the first bits.

BUFFERING

Have you ever been streaming an exciting show only to have it stop to "buffer"? You might see a loading sign. It's annoying but buffering is necessary for streaming. Buffering allows a video or other media file to load a little bit ahead of time while you watch or listen. So, if your internet connection is briefly interrupted, your video or music won't stop.

However, if the connection is slow or stops for a longer period of time, the buffer will fail and the stream will stop until enough data is downloaded to allow the stream to continue.

BUFFERING MEANS THAT A VIDEO DOESN'T NEED TO BE DOWNLOADED AT THE EXACT SAME SPEED AS SOMEONE IS VIEWING IT.

IN THE BEGINNING

THE IDEA OF BUFFERING BEGAN AT A TIME WHEN THE INTERNET WAS VERY SLOW. EVEN SMALLER DOWNLOADS TOOK A LONG TIME. BUFFERING ONE SMALL BIT OF MEDIA AT A TIME ALLOWED FASTER, SMOOTHER STREAMING. WE STILL USE BUFFERS TO PREVENT LAG EVEN THOUGH THE INTERNET IS MUCH FASTER NOW.

THE GOOD AND THE BAD

Streaming lets us play music, movies, and games whenever we want. We don't have to store them in the permanent memory on our computers. We don't have to own hundreds of CDs and DVDs. Streaming makes renting entertainment easy too—and there's no need to return what we rent.

JUST TEMPORARY

BUFFERING USES TEMPORARY, NOT PERMANENT, MEMORY. YOUR COMPUTER LOADS SMALL PIECES OF INFORMATION AT A TIME. WHEN THE INFORMATION IS USED (AS YOU WATCH OR LISTEN), THE COMPUTER "FORGETS" IT AND LOADS THE NEXT BIT COMING IN. THESE SMALL PIECES SHOULD FLOW TOGETHER SO YOU'D NEVER KNOW THE FILE WAS BROKEN UP.

One drawback of streaming media has probably happened to you. You can only stream if the internet is working. If the power turns off during a storm, for example, the movie you're watching, music you're listening to, or online game you're playing will also stop working if it's connected to the power source.

THE CONNECTION TO THE INTERNET IN YOUR HOME NEEDS A SUPPLY OF ELECTRICITY.

SERVERS

As the internet has grown, so has the number of servers. A server is a special kind of computer that can store much more than the average computer. It can send programs, services, and data to other computers around the world through the internet. As long as you have an internet connection, servers are available whenever you want.

See what's next.
WATCH ANYWHERE. CANCEL ANYTIME.

CDNs

DID YOU KNOW WHERE A SERVER IS LOCATED CAN MAKE A DIFFERENCE IN HOW FAST YOU CAN ACCESS STREAMING MEDIA? THAT'S WHY STREAMING SERVICES MAY HAVE GROUPS OF CONNECTED SERVERS IN MANY LOCATIONS AROUND THE WORLD. THESE SERVERS ARE CALLED A CONTENT DELIVERY NETWORK (CDN), OR A CONTENT DISTRIBUTION NETWORK.

AS OF 2021, NETFLIX HAD 17,000 SERVERS IN 158 COUNTRIES TO PROVIDE ITS STREAMING SERVICES. A SERVER ROOM IS PICTURED HERE.

Sites like YouTube, Spotify, and Amazon use many servers to store lots of videos, songs, and other files. You don't have to wait for a library or a store to open as people once did. You can access them at any time.

A DATA RACE

Have you ever seen a relay race? In a relay race, a team of runners takes turns racing. Each teammate runs part of the race. When the first runner finishes the first part of the race, they pass a stick called a baton to another runner. This tells the second runner it's their turn to run.

PACKETS

EACH PIECE OF STREAMING MEDIA SENT BETWEEN A SERVER AND A COMPUTER IS CALLED A PACKET. THE SIZE OF PACKETS IS DECIDED BY CERTAIN RULES. (SEE PAGE 24 TO LEARN ABOUT THESE RULES.) IF THE SIZE OF THE PACKETS WERE NOT ALL THE SAME WHEN SENDING A FILE, THE COMPUTER WOULD HAVE MORE WORK TO DO AND THE DOWNLOADS WOULD BE SLOWER, WITH MORE LAGS.

After the second runner finishes, they pass the baton to the third runner, who passes the baton to the fourth runner, and so on. Streaming is a bit like a relay race, except that pieces of information are being passed to

Streaming isn't as simple as a relay race, of course. A streaming server often has to work and connect with more than one computer at once.

WHY STREAMING PROBLEMS OCCUR

USER PROBLEMS

WI-FI ISSUES

DEVICES SLOWED BY RUNNING PROGRAMS

OLD DEVICES

TOO LITTLE BANDWIDTH ON HOME NETWORK

NETWORK PROBLEMS

DATA CONGESTION

DATA STORED FAR AWAY

KNOWING THE DIFFERENT PROBLEMS THAT CAN OCCUR CAN HELP YOU IMPROVE YOUR STREAMING EXPERIENCE.

WHAT'S WRONG?

HAVE YOU EVER HAD A PROBLEM ACCESSING THE INTERNET AND TRIED TO FIGURE IT OUT? THERE'S MORE THAN ONE REASON WHY YOU MAY NOT BE ABLE TO GET ON A WEBSITE OR STREAM A SONG. THE PROBLEM MIGHT BE SOMETHING YOU CAN SOLVE WITH YOUR INTERNET GEAR OR A NETWORK PROBLEM SOMEONE ELSE NEEDS TO FIX.

So imagine hundreds of runners with hundreds of batons running hundreds of different races. Picture the many problems that must be solved for these races to be successful. If the batons are too large and heavy, the runners will drop them. Too many runners will make the track really crowded and some may be forced to slow down or stop. In the same way, many problems need to be solved to make streaming work.

SEEKING OUT YOUR STREAM

When you own a movie, you might keep it in your own computer, on a DVD, or on a data storage device that can connect to your computer called an external drive. But when you stream the movie, someone else keeps it for you on a server. Your computer has to go find it.

This is done using web addresses called URLs (uniform resource locators). These work for computers searching for servers the same way your house address or phone number tells people how to find you and contact you. Web addresses tell computers how to find files on the internet.

ON STREAMING SERVICES, YOU PROBABLY CLICK ON AN ICON TO CHOOSE CONTENT TO STREAM RATHER THAN TYPE IN A URL. THE URL IS LINKED TO THE ICON.

WHAT'S IN A CLICK?

IF YOU RENT A MOVIE FROM A SERVICE LIKE AMAZON, YOU GO TO THE MAIN SITE AND CLICK ON THE MOVIE YOU WANT TO WATCH. THIS CONNECTS YOU TO A SERVER THAT MAY HOLD THOUSANDS OF MOVIES. THE SERVER HAS ADDRESSES THAT SHOW WHERE THE MOVIE IS. YOUR LINK TIES YOU TO THE EXACT MOVIE YOU CHOSE.

IN THE CLOUD

The servers that are accessed through the internet, and the **software** and data on those servers, are said to be "in the cloud." They aren't on your computer or other devices, but you can connect to them through the internet. You can also store your own movies, videos, music, photos, and games in the cloud. You can connect to them whenever you need to through your internet connection.

CLOUD GAMING

SOME GAMES REQUIRE YOU TO DOWNLOAD THEM ONTO YOUR COMPUTER. BUT CLOUD-BASED GAMING SERVICES ALLOW YOU TO PLAY A GAME ON ANY DEVICE THAT CONNECTS TO THE INTERNET. A PLUS OF THIS KIND OF GAMING IS THAT YOU'RE USING SOFTWARE IN THE CLOUD. SOME GAMES YOU STREAM USING THE CLOUD ARE FREE—BUT YOU NEED TO PAY MONEY TO UNLOCK CERTAIN FEATURES.

ROBLOX IS A POPULAR CLOUD-BASED GAME.

The cloud can be accessed through a web **browser** such as Chrome, Firefox, and Safari. Some companies offer special **apps** to access their services in the cloud too. When you stream media, you're probably using cloud-based technology.

PROTOCOLS

Complicated things often work better if they use simple rules to keep order. Traffic works better with traffic lights. Cars go on green and stop on red. Everyone obeys the lights, which makes everyone safer. Games, too, work better with rules.

Streaming media has rules as well. Rules for how computers communicate with each other are called protocols. Streaming first became possible through a set of rules called real-time streaming protocol (RTSP). It was developed in the late 1990s by three groups of engineers and programmers working together from Columbia University and the computer services companies called Netscape and Progressive Networks (now RealNetworks).

A HANDSHAKE CALLED AN SSL/TLS HANDSHAKE OCCURS WHEN A WEB BROWSER REACHES OUT TO A WEBSITE. THE WEBSITE PROVIDES PROOF THAT IT'S SAFE AND SECURE.

← → C 🔒 Secure | https://www.

← → C 🔒 Not Secure | http ://www.

A HANDSHAKE?

THERE ARE RULES FOR SENDING PACKETS OF INFORMATION BETWEEN SERVERS AND COMPUTERS OVER THE INTERNET. THE ARRANGEMENTS ARE SOMETIMES CALLED HANDSHAKES, AND THEY'RE A BIT LIKE PEOPLE MEETING EACH OTHER. THE TWO SIDES, YOUR COMPUTER AND A SERVER, SWAP MESSAGES TO GREET EACH OTHER, FIND OUT WHAT THE OTHER IS, AND ESTABLISH HOW THEY'LL COMMUNICATE.

Computers (and other smart devices) and servers talk to each other using RTSP to arrange data swaps of audio, video, and **animation**. RTSP also allows some control request operations, or commands, including play and pause. However, RTSP wasn't set up to do the actual transmitting of data. A different protocol did that, such as real-time transport protocol (RTP).

DESIGNED BY APPLE

THE APPLE COMPANY DESIGNED HTTP LIVE STREAMING, OR HLS, FOR ITS PRODUCTS, BUT HLS IS NOW USED ON MOST SMART DEVICES. IT PROVIDES GREAT QUALITY, BUT ISN'T IDEAL FOR SUPERFAST LIVESTREAMING. PACKETS ARE BETWEEN 5 AND 10 SECONDS, AND THE PROTOCOL OFTEN ADDS A DELAY, OR LAG, OF 20 OR MORE SECONDS TO THE STREAM.

WHEN YOU CLICK ON OR PRESS A COMMAND LIKE PAUSE, YOU'RE COMMUNICATING WITH THE SERVER THAT HOLDS THE STREAMING CONTENT.

SUBSCRIBE

As technology has changed, different protocols have taken the place of RTSP, although it hasn't completely disappeared. Today, the most widely used protocol is HTTP Live Streaming (HLS). It can be used on most devices and delivers high-quality video.

CHANGING TIMES

It's hard to overstate how much streaming has changed certain businesses. Streaming means that anyone with access to the internet has access to online media whenever they want it. For example, people once had to go to a movie theater to see a movie that just came out. Now people can see it without leaving their homes if the movie studio agrees to upload the movie to a streaming service.

The same happens with new music. Rather than buying music at a store, people can hear their favorite music on a streaming service that musicians have allowed to play their music. What will you stream today?

A STREAMING TIMELINE

1969 — THE INTERNET-LIKE NETWORK CALLED ARPANET IS ESTABLISHED.

A METHOD OF REDUCING DATA FILE SIZE PAVES THE WAY FOR VIDEO STREAMING. — **1974**

1992 — VIDEO AND AUDIO ARE SENT OVER THE INTERNET FOR THE FIRST TIME.

SEVERE TIRE DAMAGE GIVES THE FIRST LIVE ONLINE CONCERT. — **1993**

MICROSOFT CREATES A WEB BROWSER. — **1994**

1995 — THE AMAZON COMPANY GOES ONLINE FOR THE FIRST TIME.

ESPN STREAMS A LIVE RADIO BROADCAST OF A SEATTLE MARINERS AND NEW YORK YANKEES BASEBALL GAME. — **1995**

1996 — THE RULES OF STREAMING CALLED RTSP ARE CREATED.

1998 — THE GOOGLE SEARCH ENGINE BECOMES AVAILABLE.

FACEBOOK BEGINS ONLINE. — **2004**

2005 — YOUTUBE IS STARTED.

THE SPOTIFY PLATFORM IS CREATED. — **2006**

2007 — NETFLIX INTRODUCES ITS STREAMING SERVICE.

ABOUT 5 BILLION PEOPLE HAVE ACCESS TO THE INTERNET. — **2021**

STREAMING HAS COME A LONG WAY IN JUST A FEW DECADES! HERE ARE SOME NOTEWORTHY EVENTS.

PAY TO PLAY

STREAMING ONLINE IS A GREAT WAY TO SAVE MEMORY SPACE ON YOUR DEVICES, BUT THERE ARE DOWNSIDES TOO. YOU OR YOUR PARENTS MIGHT SIGN UP FOR SERVICES THAT ALLOW YOU TO STREAM. AMAZON, APPLE MUSIC, AND NETFLIX ALL CHARGE USERS FEES FOR THEIR STREAMING CONTENT. WHEN THESE FEES ADD UP, THEY CAN BE COSTLY.

GLOSSARY

access: The right or permission to use something.

animation: A video that uses drawings or graphics that appear to move when seen one after another very quickly.

app: Short for application. Computer and smartphone programs that are made to perform certain functions, or tasks.

bandwidth: A measurement of the maximum amount of data that a device or system can receive or send over the internet in an amount of time.

browser: A computer program used to locate information on the internet.

complicated: Having many pieces or stages. Also, hard to understand.

congestion: The reduction of the quality of an internet connection due to too much data being transmitted over a network.

media: Video or audio files that are stored in computers and can be played or streamed.

permanent: Lasting or unchanging.

podcast: A digital program, often involving music and speaking, that can be downloaded or streamed via the internet.

software: Programs for a computer.

technology: Using science, engineering, and other industries to invent useful tools or to solve problems. Also a machine, piece of equipment, or method created by technology.

Wi-Fi: A wireless technology in computer networks that uses radio waves to send data at high speeds over short distances.

FOR MORE INFORMATION

BOOKS

Burgan, Michael. *Netflix, Amazon, Hulu, and Streaming Video*. Broomall, PA: Mason Crest, 2019.

Eboch, M. M. *How Does Streaming Work?* North Mankato, MN: Capstone Press, 2021.

Mara, Wil. *Streaming TV*. Ann Arbor, MI: Cherry Lake Publishing, 2019.

WEBSITES

How Streaming Video and Audio Work
electronics.howstuffworks.com/tech/streaming-video-and-audio.html
Read more about how streaming works, including issues that affect the quality of content.

Living Online
pbskids.org/fetch/ruff/living-online/
Check out these videos and quizzes about kinds of technology.

Streaming Media
www.explainthatstuff.com/streamingmedia.html
Take a look at the patent for streaming media while discovering more about this fascinating technology.

INDEX